N

Written by Lee-Ann Wright

Contents

PEARSON

The Missing

Every day, all kinds of people go missing all over the world – children, teenagers, men and women of all ages and nationalities. There are many different reasons why they go missing.

The most common reasons behind the disappearance of children, teenagers and young adults are that they have had an accident, run away or someone has kidnapped or harmed them.

Adults go missing for many reasons, including illness (both mental and physical), drug and alcohol problems or as a result of a crime. Some adults choose to disappear. They break all contact with their family. They may run away when they cannot cope with certain problems in their lives. Some start new lives, while others wander the streets with nowhere to go.

Other reasons why people go missing include family violence, abuse and neglect, natural disasters, war, and even murder.

Posters of missing persons after the attacks on the World Trade Center in New York, USA, September 2001

Natural Disasters

Natural disasters, such as a tsunami, an earthquake, a volcanic eruption or a cyclone, can cause chaos in people's lives. Some people may die in the disaster; some are taken to hospital; some are rapidly evacuated to safer places. Sometimes children become separated from their parents and get lost. Many families get split up.

Luckily, when a natural disaster strikes, there are many organisations that are ready to help families find their missing loved ones.

After a disaster, the Red Cross provides people with satellite phones to try and make contact with family.

A Red Cross volunteer looks at the damage caused by the earthquake and tsunami that hit Japan in March 2011.

JAPANESE
RED CROSS SOCIETY

THE HUMANITARIAN FORUM
PROGRESS THROUGH PARTNERSHIP

The Humanitarian Forum works with organisations around the world to help tackle poverty and injustice.

COMITE INTERNATIONAL GENEVE

Refugees United

Refugees United is an organisation that helps refugees to find their families.

The mission of the International Committee of the Red Cross (ICRC) is to protect the lives of victims of disasters and is to provide them with help.

After a natural disaster, there is often a lot of damage to the surroundings. Buildings and cities may be turned into rubble. It can take days or weeks to find people who have gone missing.

Organisations like the Red Cross have specially trained staff with sophisticated technology and years of experience in finding missing people.

A lot of their work involves:
- providing aid;
- searching for and identifying bodies;
- allowing people who are searching for missing family and friends access to telephones, computers, the internet and handwritten messages;
- creating lists of missing people, especially children who have been separated from their families.

Sometimes a missing person is found quickly and a family is reunited, but sometimes finding people can take years.

A Red Cross volunteer helps a refugee make a phone call to a relative.

A young girl is returned to her family
with the help of the Red Cross.

War and Refugees

Throughout history, wars have affected millions of people. Today, not much has changed. Wars still affect many people. Soldiers and innocent people continue to lose their lives or go missing.

During World War I and II, it is estimated that more than 70 million soldiers and civilians were killed. Most soldiers wore identification tags (called dog tags), which helped identify them when they were found. But the fate of millions of others who went missing will never be known.

Today, most soldiers still wear dog tags for identification. New technology also makes it easier to track the missing soldiers.

Identification tags of missing soldiers

Many countries have memorials known as the Tomb of the Unknown Soldier. These memorials help people commemorate all the unidentified soldiers who died in the World Wars.

Millions of innocent people have been affected by war or by fighting between tribes or religious groups. Some people are unlawfully imprisoned, seriously injured or killed. Many are taken from their homes and forced to join an army. Families are split up, leaving surviving relatives not knowing where their missing family members are and whether they will ever see them again.

Posters of people missing in war are sometimes put up by family members.

In war, the Red Cross uses helicopters to transport wounded people to hospital.

Some men, women and children who manage to survive being caught up in the chaos of war have no choice but to run for their lives. They run from their homes, and everything they know, to look for a better life. These displaced people, or refugees, may flee from their own country to another country, searching for safety. Sometimes they may never return home again.

Tens of thousands of refugees from Rwanda carry their belongings as they flee towards Tanzania.

TANZANIA

RWANDA

BURUNDI

AFRICA

Sometimes the refugees end up in a neighbouring country that may be very poor. The refugees are likely to get very little help and support from the government in these places. They have to form camps, often in terrible conditions. They want desperately to start new lives, but often they face disease and starvation. Help has to come from aid organisations and from government aid programmes worldwide. These organisations can quickly provide better-equipped camps with shelter, water and food. They can help families needing medical aid or seeking to be reunited with missing family members. They will help them move to new homelands.

A refugee camp in Sudan

The Red Cross at this camp hands out essential items to refugees.

The refugees in this camp have put up shelters using anything they can find.

The Emotional Impact

When a person goes missing, no matter what the reasons, it is devastating for the family and friends who are left behind. Many find it difficult to accept. They do not know what happened to the missing person, what to do or where to turn for support. The emotions they experience may include anger, blame, guilt, doubt, fear, frustration, helplessness and loneliness.

For many, the disappearance of a loved one remains unsolved and their location unknown. They know that finding that person is never an easy task and the longer that person stays missing, the harder it becomes to find them.

Some lucky families, who finally find their missing loved ones, feel overwhelming emotions of joy and relief that their long wait is over.

A young Indian girl holds up a poster during a protest by the Association of Parents of Disappeared People (APDP). This group seeks out information on missing family members.

"Where are our dear ones?"

Index

Informational Reports

Informational Reports record factual information about a specific topic.

How to Write an Informational Report

Step One

Select a topic.
Write down the things you know about the topic.
Write down the things you need to find out.

The Missing — Research Brief

Why do people go missing?

What happens when people go missing in a natural disaster?
What do aid organisations and ordinary people do
to find missing family and friends?

What happens when people go missing in wars?
What things can people do to find missing people?

What happens when refugees end up in refugee camps?
What help can people get if their family has been split up
and needs reuniting?

What feelings do people experience when their loved ones
are missing?

Step Two

Locate the information you need.
Use different kinds of resources for your investigation:

Internet, Library, Television documentaries, Experts...

Take notes or make copies of what you find.

Sort through your notes. Organise your information using headings.

Natural Disasters

People go missing in natural disasters because they have:
* died in the disaster
* been taken away to hospitals
* been evacuated to safer places and got split up from family.

Organisations provide specially trained staff and sophisticated technology to find the missing. They can:
* search for and identify bodies
* use computers and telephones and the Internet to find the missing
* create lists of displaced people.

What feelings do people experience when their loved ones are missing?

Step Four

Use your notes to write your Report.

Include an **introduction** with an opening statement:
Every day, all kinds of people go missing all over the world – children, teenagers, men and women of all ages and nationalities. There are many different reasons why they go missing.

Include **visuals** such as…

Labels   **Captions**   **Photographs**   **Map**   **Logos**

Your Report could have…

a Contents page   **an Index**

Some reports have a Glossary.

Guide Notes

Title: Missing

Stage: Informational Report

Text Form: Informational Report

Approach: Guided Reading

Processes: Thinking Critically, Exploring Language, Processing Information

Written and Visual Focus: Labels, Captions, Index, Photographs, Contents Page, Map, Logos

THINKING CRITICALLY
(sample questions)

Before Reading – Establishing Prior Knowledge
- What do you know about why people go missing and the ways that they are found?

Visualising the Text Content
- What might you expect to see in this book?
- What form of writing do you think will be used by the author?
- Look at the Contents page and Index. Encourage the students to think about the information and make predictions about the text content.

After Reading – Interpreting the Text
- What do you think is the purpose of this book?
- How does the introduction text on pages 2–3 explain the idea behind the topic?
- What other reasons do you think might lie behind people going missing?
- Look at pages 4–5. What inferences can you make about the people who work in organisations that help reunite families after disasters?
- What do you think are the benefits of using the Internet to find families and friends in the aftermath of a disaster?
- What inferences can you make about the impact that refugees have on the countries they flee to?
- Why do you think it gets harder to find missing people after a long time?
- Why do you think people may experience guilt as an emotion when they have a loved one disappear?
- How do you think ordinary people can help the organisations dealing with refugees?
- What feelings are evoked by the photographic images in this book?
- What inferences can you make about the author from her selection of the topic?
- What questions do you have after reading the text?
- Do you think the author effectively conveyed the information in this book? Why or why not?